ADHD In The Classroom:
A Powerful, Practical Solution

ADHD In The Classroom:
A Powerful, Practical Solution

Beatrice Hair, M.A.

Founder and Director of Salisbury Tutoring Academy, Ltd.

To order additional copies of this book, contact:
staltd@vnet.net
fax request to 1-704-633-8206

23982

Contents

I DEDICATE THIS BOOK TO MY HUSBAND RANDY
FOR HIS UNCONDITIONAL LOVE AND TO
MY AUNT ELEANOR FOR HER INSPIRATION.
[DR. ELEANOR ROWE]

SHORT SUMMARY: ADHD/ADD students often create negative energy that interferes with their peers, teachers, and families. This book is designed to be a powerful and practical support tool for classroom teachers of ADHD/ADD students of any age. The goal of this workbook is to share with teachers a structure and philosophy, preparing them to help students transform negative energy into a positive and productive behavior. The contract presented here has been used successfully with more than 1,000 students. Parents, students, and teachers experience positive results with this tool. This tool can be applied to regular students for enrichment purposes.

BIO: Beatrice Hair is a child advocate, educator, author, athlete, and devoted wife. A graduate of Wake Forest University, Hair earned two degrees, including a B.A. in Education. Hair received her Masters in Curriculum and Instruction from the University of Phoenix. During her 16 year career, she has taught in the classroom and now owns and operates her school, Salisbury Tutoring Academy, LTD in Salisbury, North Carolina. In 1994, the Rowan-Salisbury Board of Education awarded Hair the CHADD Award for her outstanding work with ADHD children. Seeing the need for one-on-one instruction in 1996, Hair opened a school for students, many of whom have Attention Deficit Hyperactivity Disorder (ADHD). In 2002, Hair co-founded Salisbury's first ADHD summer camp. She often teaches workshops for teachers and parents on the subject of ADHD and positive behavior modification. Hair designed a tool that is used daily by her staff of 33 teachers to help modify student behavior.

Hair has taught hundreds of teachers how to use this tool. More than 1,000 students have experienced success due to the structure and philosophy of this contract. Parents, students, and teachers experience positive results with this tool. Hair can be reached via her school's website at *www.staltd.com.*

FOREWORD: What do ADHD students need? They crave structure, consistency, and individual attention. What do classroom teachers need? They need uninterrupted instructional time and the ability to conserve their valuable energy. This workbook is designed to address the challenges of both dilemmas and equip teachers with tools to create an accommodating educational environment for these special children. Not only does this tool command students' attention, it helps keep them motivated.

> "Never discourage anyone . . . who continuously makes progress, no matter how slow."

> Plato

Heartiest congratulations to Beatrice Hair on the publication of her first book. Parents and teachers, and most importantly, students with ADHD, will benefit from the experience and expertise she shares in this book.

Senator Elizabeth Dole

I have co-taught with Beatrice in her workshops for teachers. She provides tools that work. Her approach is insightful and practical. She is energetic and connects with students and teachers alike.

Jill Aiken, M.D.
Pediatrician for ADHD

Teachers need this tool; they need an effective, simple, easy behavior modification contract that has been proven effective in different schools for multi-ages. This tool is a powerful way to know whether successful behavior management has been achieved.

Wayne C. Koontz, M.D.
Pediatrician for ADHD

Mrs. Hair has the rare ability to translate theory into practical application. "ADHD In the Classroom: A Powerful, Practical

Solution" is a must read for teachers and parents of ADHD students.

James Connelly, Ed.D.
Professor—University of Phoenix

I work with Mrs. Hair and know how passionate she is about this program. It's a stimulating and innovative tool that helps all types of students succeed. This exceptional book should be used by all educators.

Debbie J. Beck
National Board Certified Teacher
Teacher-of-the-Year

A fine teacher in her own right, Beatrice Hair has put together a clear, goal-oriented approach to dealing with ADHD that parents and educators should find helpful.

Elizabeth G. Cook
Editor, Salisbury Post

As parents of two sons with ADHD, we can attest that the greatest share of our behavioral issues revolve around school. The tool is simple enough for any of us, whether teacher, parent, or student to understand and use. It has enabled us to work as a team with a tremendous positive impact.

Susan DeCamp and Gary Freeze, Ph.D.
Salisbury Tutoring Academy, LTD Parents

Acknowledgements

I owe many thanks to many people who have been instrumental in the implementation of this behavior modification tool and in the writing of this book. I feel grateful to each of the more than 1,000 parents who worked with me, making this tool effective. My heartfelt appreciation goes to the 33 teachers on my staff who diligently maintain the integrity and consistency of this tool. I feel, above all else, that it is a great privilege to be an integral part of so many students' lives and their experience with success.

I feel indebted to my friend Patricia Hinson, for encouraging me to write this book. I am thankful to my long time friend Rosemary Martin for her contribution to the writing process. I will always feel the deepest love for my husband, Randy Hair, for the many years of support and encouragement as I founded and developed my school. Lastly, I would like to thank Becky Smith, my graduate school friend, for her editing skills and humor.

I am grateful to Gina Pittard, M.D. for years of sharing ADHD medical information and for our special friendship. I thank Jon E. Palmer for his enthusiastic help in designing the cover art, and Jillian McCartney for her diligent editing skills.

I trust this book will help make life a little better for teachers, students, and parents.

Introduction

How often have teachers conducted a parent-teacher conference where both the teacher and parent complain about the student and no game plan is established to improve the situation? This book is designed to accomplish several goals. It should help the classroom teacher gain insight into a powerful tool that has been used successfully in Salisbury, North Carolina with more than 1,000 students. The teacher will learn how to design behavior modification contracts with individual goals centered on the six major behaviors he/she wants the students to modify. Teachers will gain skills in developing effective behavior modification contracts to include time frames involved, the incentives, and the consequences. Samples of contracts, journaling, and visual aids will be used to facilitate learning. This tool is applicable for students of all ages and various age-appropriate examples are provided. The contract commands students' attention and keeps them motivated.

Workbook Overview

A. The intended audience of this workbook is certified teachers who have ADHD (Attention Deficit Hyperactivity Disorder) students in their classrooms; however this tool can be used in many different ways at home or by a tutor.

B. The context of this contract is to help modify the behaviors of ADHD students in a positive way.
C. The tool in this workbook is a behavior chart that combines a powerful incentive and consequence philosophy.
D. The teachers using this workbook feel both compassion and frustration toward their ADHD/ADD student.
E. The teachers will lead the situation out of a frustrating frame into a positive problem-solving realm.
F. The teachers will begin a healing process for their students' ADHD symptoms.

What Will Teachers Learn?

A. The teachers will learn how to use an individual behavior modification contract.
B. The teachers will be able to individually apply this contract to different students.

The goal of this workbook is for teachers to learn skills to help modify ADHD behavior. The teachers will use a behavior modification tool to monitor and reward positive changes in students' behavior; consequences will be used when needed. This workbook includes three different learning goals: cognitive, psychomotor, and affective. The cognitive goal involves learning how to apply the contract. The psychomotor goal includes learning the different ways to manipulate the contract. The affective goal is to change negative attitudes toward ADHD.

Basic Strategy

This contract will include the three-legged table philosophy by requiring supportive roles from the teacher, parent, and student. This philosophy states that if one leg on a three-legged table is broken or weak, the table will not stand. The parent, teacher, and student need to each follow through with their own responsibilities. This guideline will guarantee the success of the contract; however, a contract is only as good as the commitment of all the people who sign it.

1. Why was this performance measurement method selected?
   ADHD/ADD students crave structure, individual attention, and consistency.
2. What are the relevant advantages and disadvantages of this measurement method?
   The relevant advantage of using the contract is that it teaches students that hard work pays. A fair warning is that without a strong commitment from all three parties, the contract might not be successful. All three parties must work together, and all parties must understand their respective roles.
3. Who should care about the results of the performance measurements?
   Everyone will benefit if the contract is successful. The students receive incentives, the teacher has a more positive climate in the classroom, and the parent receives support while trying to raise a responsible citizen and family member. The healing process begins for everyone.
4. Why should they care?

The teacher

The teacher will have less stress dealing with the ADHD student in the classroom. The classroom teacher has limited time to deal with negative behaviors during instructional time. This contract will help the teacher be more effective and efficient. Once the contract is signed, checking it off takes less than a minute.

The student

The student can be proud of the incentives earned and will experience improved self-esteem. Students enjoy the guarantee of the individual attention by the teacher.

The parent

The parent will observe improved behavior and self-esteem.

Journal Writing Prompts

- Describe the risks to the classroom environment of not using a behavior modification plan with ADHD students.

- Describe possible ideas for reasonable consequences and incentives.

Incentives

Incentives (continued)

Incentives (continued)

Consequences

Consequences (continued)

Consequences (continued)

- Describe the top six behaviors in ADHD students that need modification.

Student 1

Student 2

Student 3

Student 4

Student 5

Student 6

Student 7

Student 8

Student 9

Student 10

This contract can be used to motivate a brilliant student, to help a low student, and with students of all ages.

Problem: Johnny is a middle school student who does not bring a pencil to class. He interrupts others, does not do his homework, and often lays his head on his desk during class. He has trouble with math because he does not know his multiplication facts yet.

Solution: Design the following contract with these goals and check daily.

Sample Contract

Hair's Behavior Modification Contract for: _Johnny_

GOALS	DATES							
Bring materials								
Raise hand and wait to speak								
Know math fact cards								
Keep head up during class								
Bring completed homework								

Weekly Treats Include: _Allowance + 1 dollar per goal -2 per miss_

Completed Contract Treats Include: _Ski trip after 3 contracts!_

You May Miss __3__ Stickers per Contract   _Consequence per miss - one day of no T.V._

You May Miss ___ Contracts

Teacher: _____
Student: _____
Parent: _____

Instructional Strategies and Rationale

There are no quick fixes when it comes to ADHD. Teachers should expect that student behavior will be modified slowly over time. The question of "What should I do with this child?" will be answered. The North Carolina Department of Public Instruction states that teachers are responsible for reaching their ADHD students. The federal standard of *No Child Left Behind* includes ADHD students as one of the categories (NCDPI, 2002). Not only must the students be taught, they must also be stopped from disrupting the education of others.

Getting Started: The Incentives

Teachers must remember that ADHD students may need structure, medication, academic modification, and behavior modification. Many ADHD students are also very gifted and need to have outlets for their talents: sports, drama, music, etc. ADHD students' *behavior* irritates others; however, most ADHD students internalize that others do not like *them*.

The first step is to sit down with the student and request a wish list. Many students know what they want. At this point, the teacher's role becomes that of an advocate for the student, conveying the message of being the student's ally. The teacher will then schedule a power meeting with the parents and negotiate for the student's incentives. Examples of incentives and consequences that can be used to help the student brainstorm ideas:

- Trip to theme park with a friend
- Sleep-over
- Game boy (give them things they like!)
- Movies
- Special dinner at students' favorite restaurant with family, friends, or both
- Allowance
- Music CD
- Special privileges (at the high school level this may involve car privileges)
- Special trip to mountains, beach, athletic event
- Fishing trip with Dad (attention is always a good incentive)
- For high school students: later curfews, a car, accessories for the car
- Manicure, pedicure, massage, or facial

Consequences

Consequences may be anything a teacher or parent can use as leverage. For example, one middle school student lost the privilege of wearing his favorite shoes to school. For high school students, driving and curfew privileges can be curtailed on the weekends.

Consequences should be reasonable and consistent:

- Loss of privileges—Be specific. Examples: no television for one day, no Nintendo, no phone or no music.

- No allowance—The students may also owe by subtracting money for missed goals. For example, students can earn $1 for an earned sticker/goal, and they would lose $2 per missed goal. It is recommended that colorful markers or stickers be used to symbolize accomplished goals on the contract.
- Extra household chores—With this consequence, students usually decide for themselves that they would rather meet the goals than do extra chores. Chore ideas include: clean cars, windows, bathrooms, rake leaves, or wash dishes.

The Power Meeting

The purpose of the power meeting is to save time in the long run. This is where the three-legged-table philosophy is conveyed and the negotiations begin. In order to conduct an effective parent/teacher/student conference, teachers may use this as a checklist:

- Consequences need to be reasonable, specific, and loving.
- Consequences should not be overwhelming. Force and pressure causes the paralysis of growth. For example, one missed goal should result in one day of no television, rather than a week.
- Allow a designated number of missed goals (3-8) without any consequences to allow a child to be a child.
- There is a fine line between holding a standard and being overbearing. Misses must be allowed matter-of-factly without parents "bearing down" on the students.
- Do not over-punish or under-punish. Many parents ignore behaviors for too long and then explode.
- Offer positive incentives with total consistency.
- Incentives must be offered on time because children do not understand excuses. As an analogy, an employer cannot explain that an employee's paycheck is not ready because the employer's grandmother is in the hospital.

- Do not give incentives early. Again, if an employer offers the employee a paycheck early, it may lessen motivation.
- The contract operates on this paycheck basis. As adults, even if we love our jobs, we could easily find other things we would rather do with our time. A paycheck motivates us to stay committed.
- Incentives help provide healing to psychic wounds; often ADHD students have been hurting for years.
- Encourage parents to make the first incentive inviting to the student to help the student buy into the solution more quickly. Be sure to refer to their list. Example: ski trip, shopping spree, or a new outfit.
- Parents need to use caution in offering incentives. The incentive must be an item that is available in stores, in season, etc., so that it will be delivered on time.
- Parents should **give** their children less material goods and privileges to allow them to **earn** more instead.
- Parents, students, and teachers need to agree and sign the contract. This way the student commits to being a part of the solution. Everyone should receive a copy of the signed contract.
- Students need to have individual instructional plans that allow for academic modifications, separate from this tool.
- Students also need to be under the regular care of a physician experienced in managing children with ADHD/ ADD. Medication options may be used in conjunction with this contract.
- Parents need to coordinate with the grandparents, spouses, ex-spouses or significant others to explain the agreement and avoid misinterpretation of the incentive understanding. For example, other family members should not inadvertently give the contracted incentive to the student as a birthday present or for another occasion.
- Parents need to provide additional praise when students receive all of their stickers.
- When issuing a consequence, remind parents not to throw

away their "big stick." For example, instead of not allowing a child to play sports for the whole season, allow the privilege of playing in the weekly games to be earned on a weekly basis.

What to do When Parental Support is Missing

In cases where teachers are not able to count on the parents for consistent incentives, they can create their own incentive system:

- Homework passes
- Extra PE with another class or recess time
- Candy (caution concerning obesity or other health issues)
- Gift certificates to something to which they have access
- Anything that will give students extra attention or the limelight (student-of-the-month or privilege of passing out papers)
- An extra trip to the treasure box

Possible school consequences if there is no parental support:

- Loss of recess or free time (or build in an extra PE class to use as leverage)
- Extra assignments
- Loss of any privileges in the classroom for the next day
- Sentence writing

A Positive Tone

The goals need to be worded in a positive way. For example, instead of saying, "No hitting your neighbor," one might say "Show kindness to your neighbor." The writing style is an important component to the success of the contract. This emphasizes the idea of making lifestyle changes and seeing goodness as a way of being. Positive wording is much more effective and sets the tone for the contract. Example:

Negative:

- No hitting your neighbor
- No back-talking
- No procrastination—taking too much time to begin working

Positive:

- Show kindness to your neighbor; it is better with little children to allow one verbal warning before consequences start.
- Speak respectfully to others.
- Get ready before teacher countdown is over; countdowns can be up (1, 2, 3) or down (3, 2, 1).
- Study math flashcards nightly.

Retros

This approach allows students to earn back a previous goal that was missed through no fault of their own. This means that a student can earn back that goal retroactively the next time the contract is checked. For example, a student needs to obtain parental signatures in the homework pad each night. The student actually did go to the parents to obtain their signature each night; however, the father kept the book-bag in the car that was taken to the shop. In this case, the student receives a "retro" goal and will have to furnish the homework pad the next time he acquires his stickers. The goals will be retroactively checked for the previous week.

Summary Pointers

Teachers will need to keep the following concepts in mind before designing their behavior modification tool:

- The behavior modification tool can be used in many different ways for home, school, or with a tutor.
- Eight weeks is a reasonable time period for an incentive. When using this tool with children under the age of six, an incentive every four weeks works best.
- Allow a minimum of three misses per eight weeks and a maximum of eight.
- The tool can be used with a daily incentive, such as allowance for a middle school student. Remember to subtract money for losses.
- It can be used with a long-term goal, such as a high school student completing three contracts to earn a car.
- It can be checked-off daily or be done once a week.
- Colorful stickers or checkmarks help; gaps in the contract work as visual reminders to motivate students.
- Using additional praise with stickers is vital.
- When a student misses a goal, the emphasis must be on the changes to be made. For example: "Johnny, you missed your back-talking goal this week. What can you do to reach this goal next week?"

Final Journaling

When this workbook is completed, the teachers will be able to incorporate the three-legged table philosophy for successful behavior modification specific to each student. Conducting an effective power meeting for all three parties is crucial. Journaling notes need to include what was most effective and ineffective about different power meetings. It is also important to document what types of incentives worked for different types of students; these journal entries can be used as references over the years.

Most effective power meeting

Most ineffective power meeting

Effective incentives

Effective consequences

Ineffective incentives

Effective consequences

- How is it best to use the contract for an eight-week period of time, daily, weekly and for the whole academic year?

Time frames that work best

How to use the contract for the duration of the year

In Review-Five
Success Steps

Step 1: Write a list the reasons why the ADHD student's disruptive behavior needs to be addressed.

Step 2: List the six major undesirable behaviors in journal space provided by this workbook.

Step 3: Design a contract specific to the student's needs.

Step 4: Conduct the power meeting and secure commitments and signatures.

Step 5: Maintain consistency.

The author of this workbook has produced a video that is used at the Salisbury Tutoring Academy, LTD to explain the guidelines of Hair's Behavior Modification Contract to the parents. This video can be ordered by contacting the academy at 818 Corporate Circle, Salisbury, N.C. 28147. Her email is *staltd@vnet.net* and her school's website is *www.staltd.com*. The school's fax is 704-633-8206.

Hair's Contract

Hair's Behavior Modification Contract for: _____

GOALS	DATES							

Weekly Treats Include: _____

Completed Contract Treats Include: _____

You May Miss ___ Stickers per Contract

You May Miss ___ Contracts

Teacher: _____

Student: _____

Parent: _____

Hair's Contract

Hair's Behavior Modification Contract for: _____

GOALS	DATES							

Weekly Treats Include: _____

Completed Contract Treats Include: _____

You May Miss ___ Stickers per Contract

You May Miss ___ Contracts

Teacher: _____

Student: _____

Parent: _____

References

North Carolina Department of Public Instruction. (2003). New federal targets tough to meet. pp. 1-2. Retrieved on July 19, 2003, from http://www.ncpublicschools.org/curriculum/computer.skills/index.html

Rothwell, W., Kazanas, H.C., Palloff, R.M., Pratt, K., Smith, P.L., & Ragan, T.J. (2002). Instructional Design. [University of Phoenix Custom Edition eBook]. New York: John Wiley & Sons.